Secretary of Homeland
Security
AR PTS
1.0
AR RL
7.7
69815

America's Leaders

SECRETARY
of Homeland Security

by Donna Schaffer
and Alfred Meyer

BLACKBIRCH®
PRESS

THOMSON

GALE

San Diego • Detroit • New York • San Francisco • Cleveland • New Haven, Conn. • Waterville, Maine • London • Munich

© 2003 by Blackbirch Press™. Blackbirch Press™ is an imprint of The Gale Group, Inc., a division of Thomson Learning, Inc.

Blackbirch Press™ and Thomson Learning™ are trademarks used herein under license.

For more information, contact
The Gale Group, Inc.
27500 Drake Rd.
Farmington Hills, MI 48331-3535
Or you can visit our Internet site at http://www.gale.com

ALL RIGHTS RESERVED
No part of this work covered by the copyright hereon may be reproduced or used in any form or by any means—graphic, electronic, or mechanical, including photocopying, recording, taping, Web distribution or information storage retrieval systems—without the written permission of the publisher.

Every effort has been made to trace the owners of copyrighted material.

Photo credit: cover, back cover © Creatas; airport security cover inset © AP WideWorld; page 4 © Blackbirch Press Archives; Tom Ridge cover inset, pages 5, 6, 7, 9, 10, 14, 13, 15, 16, 17, 18, 22, 24, 27, 30, 31 © CORBIS; pages 11 © PhotoDisc; page 12 © Corel Corporation; pages 19, 20, 25 © Getty Images

LIBRARY OF CONGRESS CATALOGING-IN-PUBLICATION DATA

Schaffer, Donna.
  Secretary of Homeland Security / by Donna E. Schaffer and Alfred Meyer.
    v. cm. — (America's leaders series)
Includes bibliographical references and index.
Contents: President's cabinet — A time of crisis — The director's responsibilities — Who works with the director? — Where does the director work? — Who is Tom Ridge? — Accomplishments so far — A new Department of Homeland Security — The first secretary of the Department of Homeland Security.
  ISBN 1-56711-960-3 (alk. paper)
  1. United States. Dept. of Homeland Security—Juvenile literature. [1. United States. Dept. of Homeland Security.] I. Meyer, Alfred. II. Title. III. Series.

HV6432.S34 2003
353.3'2293'0973—dc21   2002156280

Table of Contents

A Position Created from Tragedy

Written in 1787, the U.S. Constitution defined the rights of citizens and the basic rules that would govern the new country. The government was divided into three branches—the executive, the legislative, and the judicial. As leader of the executive branch, the president had the power to direct the government. It was also his job to carry out the laws passed by the legislature. The legislative branch was made up of the House of Representatives and the Senate, together called Congress. The court system, or judiciary, made sure that the nation's laws followed the guidelines established by the Constitution.

The Constitution defined the basic rules that govern the United States.

Congress established the State Department in 1789 to help the president maintain good relations with foreign countries.

The first Congress set up three departments to help the first president, George Washington. The State Department took care of relations with other countries. The Treasury Department managed the nation's money. The War Department was in charge of the armed forces.

USA Fact

In French, the word *cabinet* means a small council room or chamber. The use of the word to describe the group of department secretaries was probably coined in George Washington's time.

The head of each department was given the title of "Secretary." The president nominated the secretaries, but the Senate had to approve his choices. Along with an attorney general who gave advice about the law, the secretaries formed a team that became known as the president's cabinet. Cabinet members advised the president on issues that were related to their departments.

Tom Ridge became a member of the president's cabinet when he was appointed the first secretary of homeland security in January 2003.

Throughout the nation's history, new departments were sometimes added. Other times, departments were done away with. Because of this, the size of the cabinet changed many times. By the end of 2002, the total number of cabinet members was 22. The most recent addition to the cabinet was the secretary of homeland security. Unlike most other cabinet positions, this secretary's job was created in response to a terrible tragedy.

A Time of Crisis

As the 21st century began, the United States looked forward to a new period of peace. The nation was the most powerful in the world. The economy was strong, and the future looked bright. Even so, there was some cause for concern. In 1999, the U.S. Commission on National Security/21st Century warned that Americans would likely die on U.S. soil—perhaps in large numbers—in terrorist attacks. The commission also said the government was not ready to prevent such attacks or respond very well if one happened.

The World Trade Center towers in New York City were destroyed after a terrorist attack on September 11, 2001.

The commission's warning proved to be accurate. On September 11, 2001, two U.S. airliners, hijacked by Middle Eastern terrorists, slammed into the twin towers of the World Trade Center in New York City. Within just hours, these symbols of American wealth and opportunity crumbled to the ground. Meanwhile, a third hijacked airliner smashed into the nation's military headquarters, the Pentagon, in Arlington, Virginia. Finally, a fourth hijacked plane crashed in a field near Shanksville, Pennsylvania. It did not reach its target, which may have been the U.S. Capitol or the White House. In all, nearly 3,000 people died in the attacks, including many rescue workers.

USA FACT

Even though the September 11 attacks took the United States by surprise, the government was able to respond almost immediately in some ways. The Department of Defense began air patrols, and the Department of Transportation stopped all private air traffic. The president issued an order to give emergency money to New York City.

Just nine days after September 11, President George W. Bush announced that an Office of Homeland Security (OHS) had been formed. Its task was to make the country safe from future assaults, including attacks by hijacked planes or even weapons of mass destruction.

Tom Ridge (second from left) was the governor of Pennsylvania when he was chosen by the president to be the director of homeland security.

Bush selected Tom Ridge, then governor of Pennsylvania, to become the new office's director. As a member of the White House staff, Ridge would report to the president. After Ridge resigned as governor, he started his new job on October 8, 2001.

A little more than a week later, another crisis arose. A Florida man died of anthrax, a rare infectious disease spread mostly by cattle and sheep. Then, envelopes that held anthrax germs mixed with white powder arrived in the mail at a Senate office building in Washington, D.C. The government quickly closed the building and a central post office to disinfect them. Five deaths resulted from the disease.

Technicians wore protective clothing to investigate the anthrax attacks in the aftermath of the September 11 attacks. The Office of Homeland Security coordinated the investigation with the FBI, the CDC, and local authorities.

People were anxious to learn who was behind this biological incident. Many wondered if more anthrax attacks were on the way. Just days after he took office, Ridge called together the attorney general and the director of the Federal Bureau of Investigation (FBI). He also contacted scientists from the Centers for Disease Control (CDC). He hoped these people could find out who was behind the attacks. The source of the anthrax still remains a mystery, though.

The anthrax attacks, like the events of September 11, showed that Americans faced many possible dangers right in their own backyard. Besides biological incidents, these terrorist dangers included chemical and even nuclear attacks. It would be the duty of the Office of Homeland Security—and especially, its director—to help protect the United States against any future threats.

The OHS Opens for Business

The director of the OHS would not only advise and assist the president on security matters. He would also have two broad tasks. As director, Ridge's first duty was to set up a group of government employees whose main job would be to detect threats early. His second task would be to prevent terrorist attacks on U.S. soil. Ridge's top goals were to improve airport safety and to keep track of foreigners who entered the country.

> ### USA Fact
>
> Potential terrorist targets dot the American landscape. These include 429 airports, 250 major sports arenas and stadiums, almost 600,000 bridges, and 14 large dams (9 of which produce electricity). The nation also has 2,800 power plants (68 of them nuclear), 190,000 miles of natural-gas pipeline, and an undisclosed number of water treatment plants and reservoirs.

One of Tom Ridge's top goals was to improve airport safety.

The Hoover Dam, located on the border between Nevada and Arizona, is a potential terrorist target.

Even when the OHS was first created, the president hoped to eventually add a cabinet-level Department of Homeland Security. This department would take the place of the OHS. Like other departments, it would be run by a secretary. Connecticut senator Joseph Lieberman had suggested such a department even before September 11. It was only after the terrorist attacks that the president came to agree with the idea, though, and he wanted to design his own plan to set up the department.

As OHS director, it was up to Ridge to fill in many details of the president's plan. This was a tough job. Ridge had to organize the new department and figure out how much money would be needed to run it. He also had to help win over any members of Congress and the Bush administration who did not like certain parts of the president's plan.

The OHS Director and His Staff

Ridge began his job in 2001 with a staff of five, but that number grew quickly. A year later, his office had more than 150 workers.

Bush also set up a Homeland Security Council to help guide the director. It included members of the cabinet and the heads of government agencies. Experts from outside the government also participated. The council met as often as twice a week.

Tom Ridge's first meeting with the Homeland Security Council was held in the White House in October 2001.

Tom Ridge briefed President George W. Bush daily in the Oval Office.

The council then appointed more than 20 committees to explore urgent matters that the OHS faced. Transportation safety was one issue. Another was the possible terrorist use of weapons of mass destruction, including chemical, biological, and nuclear weapons. The challenge was to come up with a national strategy right away. The plan would have to keep the nation safe from terrorism even when the source of many threats lay far outside the country's borders. The council and its committees, along with daily Oval Office security briefings, kept the director informed of brewing threats in foreign lands.

The OHS Director's Office

As OHS director, Ridge was given an office just steps from the president's own in the West Wing of the White House. Many of Ridge's OHS staff worked in the nearby Executive Office Building. Others worked away from downtown Washington at an OHS security-monitoring center. The center collected all information about terror-related threats and natural disasters. Ridge visited the center often. He also set up a hotline between the center and his own White House office.

Ridge traveled the country to meet with state and local officials. He went to conferences on how to prepare for emergencies. He also made many trips to the U.S. Capitol.

The OHS staff worked in the Executive Office Building (pictured) located near the White House.

Tom Ridge met with many government officials like Speaker of the House Dennis Hastert (right) to discuss how the Department of Homeland Security would operate.

Although it is rare for a presidential appointee to testify before Congress, Ridge was often called by different House or Senate committees. They wanted him to answer questions about how the proposed Department of Homeland Security would work.

Ridge also began to plan just where such a department's headquarters would be built. Possible sites included suburban Virginia and Maryland, as well as the District of Columbia. If Congress approved the creation of the department, the building would need to have office space for the new secretary and a large staff.

The president said that even when the new Department of Homeland Security was created, he would keep an Office of Homeland Security in the White House. Its director would report only to him. The new secretary, on the other hand, would have to report to both the president and Congress.

Accomplishments of the OHS Director

Tom Ridge led the government's efforts to make air travel safer and to watch borders and their crossings more closely. At the same time, he alerted the public to many other risks. He stressed that nuclear power plants, water supplies, and public transportation systems might all be terrorist targets. He urged Americans always to be prepared.

Tom Ridge worked hard to make air travel safer by increasing security in airports.

Tom Ridge recommended that the Border Patrol be added to the Department of Homeland Security.

Ridge worked especially hard in the area of border control. He suggested that all federal agencies related to the border be combined into the new Department of Homeland Security. These agencies include, among others, the Border Patrol, the Immigration and Naturalization Service (INS), and the Federal Emergency Management Agency (FEMA). Some of the departments strongly resisted the idea. Part of the reason Bush hoped to create the new department, however, was to make sure all efforts to keep the nation safe would work together. The president pointed out that up to 100 different offices were responsible for some part of homeland security. One of the new department's most important goals would be to coordinate their work. This would help make sure one agency would be the final authority on national safety issues.

Finally, because many warnings about possible terrorist acts were often confusing, Ridge came up with a color-coded alert system. Many people criticized it at first. Still, the system was adopted. It was used on the first anniversary of September 11 to warn people that the risk of another terrorist attack was high.

A color-coded alert system was one of the first things Tom Ridge created to help warn people about possible attacks.

A New Department of Homeland Security

On June 18, 2002, Bush officially asked Congress to pass the Homeland Security Act of 2002. This law would create a Department of Homeland Security. If the act passed, a secretary would be chosen to head the department and would join the cabinet. Once nominated by the president and approved by the Senate, the new secretary would answer to both the president and Congress. The secretary's decisions could

President George W. Bush signed the Homeland Security Act into law in November 2002.

then be reviewed by as many as 88 congressional committees.

Congress debated the act over the summer and into the fall of 2002. The Republican-controlled House of Representatives approved the act in midsummer. The Democrat-controlled Senate, however, held back. Mainly, Democrats disliked the president's demand that employees of the department be denied membership in federal unions. After Republicans gained control of the Senate in the November elections, the Senate approved the act on November 19. The president signed the act into law in the Oval Office a week later, on November 25.

USA Fact

As the first director of Homeland Security, Tom Ridge was determined to make the nation as safe as possible without taking away any of the people's rights. Some critics have said that the office has harmed civil liberties. Ridge, though, said in September 2002 that he thought his department had done a good job of balancing freedom with security.

According to the law, the mission of the Department of Homeland Security is to make America safer from terrorist attacks. It was also designed to keep damage from terrorist attacks to a minimum, and to make sure that recovery from any attacks that do occur is quick and effective. Four divisions within the department will help achieve its mission.

The Coast Guard is part of the Border and Transportation division of the Department of Homeland Security.

The first is Border and Transportation Security. To tighten border control and increase security of the nation's air, land, and water transportation systems, this division will monitor who and what enters the country. To do so, it will take over several agencies, such as the Coast Guard and the Immigration and Naturalization Service. The division will also create and enforce a new high-tech visa system to better identify foreign visitors, especially those who may have terrorist plans. The system will also make sure all visitors obey the terms of their stay.

The second division is Emergency Preparedness and Response. This part of the department will work to help citizens and communities avoid becoming victims of terrorism and to swiftly aid those who do. A top priority is to put in place a reliable nationwide communications network to coordinate the tasks of those who respond first to attacks or other disasters.

The third division is Science and Technology. Its main mission is to prepare for and respond to the terrorist use of weapons of mass destruction. As the anthrax scare showed, these weapons can have terrible effects. The division would come up with ways to prevent the use of these weapons. It would also work on methods to lessen their effects if they are used.

The fourth division is Information Analysis and Infrastructure Protection. This branch will gather and study terrorist-related data from the Central Intelligence Agency (CIA), National Security Agency (NSA), and the FBI. (The CIA, NSA, and FBI will remain independent, but they will share their information with the new department.) If the information shows that an attack seems likely, the division will inform the secretary and the president. It will issue an alert and take defensive action. Protection of the nation's infrastructure is also a key part of this division's work. The infrastructure is made up of systems that range from agriculture, energy,

The Information Analysis and Infrastructure Protection division of the Department of Homeland Security obtains information from the CIA (pictured) and other government organizations to identify potential terrorist attacks.

and transportation to banking, computer networks, and telecommunications.

In all, the Department of Homeland Security will take over some 22 different federal agencies in its first two years. The budget for its first year—2003—was set at nearly $36 billion. Once the location of the new headquarters building is decided, the building itself and the land on which it is to be built will cost about $600 million. The department will employ about 170,000 workers. This will make it the third largest department in the government, smaller only than the Defense Department and the Department of Veteran's Affairs.

The First Secretary of the Department of Homeland Security

Moments before he signed the Homeland Security act into law, Bush nominated OHS Director Tom Ridge as secretary and expressed great satisfaction with the work Ridge had already done. The Senate confirmed his choice on January 22, 2003. As director of the OHS, Ridge's main task was to plan for the creation of the Department of Homeland Security. His new job as secretary of homeland security would be just a bit different. Now, he would not only plan how to fight terrorism and reorganize the government, but would actually put his ideas into practice. He would continue his work with border security and would constantly look for ways to make the nation safer.

President George W. Bush swore in OHS Director Tom Ridge as the first secretary of homeland security in January 2003.

The Secretary's Days

The secretary of homeland security is kept very busy by the mission to protect the nation against possible threats. Here is what a day might be like for the secretary.

5:00 AM	Listens to news
5:30 AM	Reads newspapers and overnight E-mail
6:00 AM	Arrives at White House office
7:15 AM	Attends security briefing by directors of the CIA and FBI in Oval Office
7:30 AM	Attends daily meeting with White House senior staff
8:00 AM	Briefs the president on current homeland security issues
8:45 AM	Confers with his deputy secretary
9:15 AM	Attends a meeting of the U.S. Conference of Mayors
10:45 AM	Works on refining strategy for Department of Homeland Security
12:00 PM	Lunch with secretary of defense and attorney general to discuss intelligence-gathering methods and results

Tom Ridge talked to workers at Ground Zero in New York after the terrorist attack on the World Trade Center.

1:00 PM	Travels to the OHS security monitoring center in northwest Washington, D.C. to meet with staff
2:15 PM	Arranges for a meeting with Canadian officials on border control
2:30 PM	Attends meeting with head of the Office of Cyberspace about defense against possible attacks on the Internet and computer networks nationwide
3:30 PM	Attends press conference with homeland security spokesperson
4:00 PM	Returns phone calls from members of Congress
5:00 PM	Dines with co-workers; leaves for home
8:00 PM	Calls office for messages and returns them

Fascinating Facts

The Changing Cabinet

As the nation grew, new departments were made, others mixed with older ones, and some were dropped. For example, the Department of the Navy was created in 1798 when the United States was threatened at sea by French and British warships and even by pirates. After World War II, President Harry Truman combined the Department of War and the Department of the Navy and added the air force as another branch of the military. He created the new Department of Defense. In 1970, President Richard M. Nixon turned the Post Office Department into a separate government body, the U.S. Postal Service. This meant that the postal service was no longer part of the cabinet.

Dimensions of the Homeland

It is the job of the secretary of homeland security to protect America's people (about 285 million), territory (3.4 million square miles), and national landmarks. The secretary also tries to ensure the safety of more than 360 seaports along the nation's 95,000 miles of seashore, and the nation's borders. The border with Canada stretches for 5,525 miles, and the border with Mexico runs nearly 2,000 miles. At least 350 legal entry points at these and other borders let people and vehicles come into the country. More than 500 million people enter the United States each year, and about 350 million of them are not U.S. citizens.

First Responders

Although the Department of Homeland Security is a national agency, it is keenly interested in local matters. One of the secretary's major goals is to give as much support as possible to so-called first responders. These local officials include firefighters, police, emergency medical technicians (EMTs), and other medical workers. The Department of Homeland Security works to give funding, training, and other help to these people, to make them better prepared to save lives if a terrorist attack happens.

Other Homeland Security Jobs

The Department of Homeland Security was created specifically to protect the nation against terrorists. Even so, it does have other jobs. This is mainly because so many different government agencies were combined to create the new department. Some of the secretary of homeland security's assignments are to handle responses to natural disasters, to try to stop money counterfeiters, and to prevent drug smuggling.

Glossary

briefing—a meeting held to provide information or news

commission—a group formed to carry out a certain task or a government agency that supervises an ongoing activity

cyberspace—the realm in which electronic information exists or is exchanged, as in e-mails

infrastructure—large-scale systems, services, and facilities of a country or region, including electric power, water supplies, public transportation, and communications

security—safety and protection against attack from without or from within

testify—to make factual statements

Tom Ridge met with Canadian prime minister Jean Chretien (left) in December 2001 about strengthening security along the border between Canada and the United States.

For More Information

Publications

Feinberg, Barbara Silberdick. *The National Government.* New York: Franklin Watts, 1993.

Parker, Nancy Winslow. *The President's Cabinet and How It Grew.* New York: HarperCollins, 1991.

Tom Ridge's job as secretary of homeland security is to protect the United States from future attacks.

Web Sites

www.whitehouse.gov/homeland

Provides news on both the Office and the Department of Homeland Security, including chats and speeches by first Homeland Security Director Tom Ridge

www.whitehouse.gov/government
This site offers detailed information about the president and his administration, and features profiles of top executives and cabinet members

www.firstgov.gov
Most government Web sites can be searched through this address

Index